Vintage Vegan

Vintage Vegan

Recipes From the World's First Raw Vegan Restaurant

Vera Richter

Plexus, London

Contents

NOTE ABOUT THE AUTHOR:
MRS VERA RICHTER

Mrs Vera Richter, along with her husband, who became known as Dr John T. Richter, opened America's first vegan, raw food restaurant, in Los Angeles in 1917. In a time when veganism and raw food never crossed the forefront of a typical American's mind, Dr and Mrs Richter established this pioneering restaurant. The restaurant itself was named The Eutropheon, meaning 'place of good nourishment' in Greek, and remained open for around twenty-five years, seating up to 350 people by 1940. Rumour has it that the restaurant was frequented by a number of stars of the period, drawn to the health benefits that the restaurant advocated. Greta Garbo was amongst the stars and is thought to have 'rejoiced in the vital foods there.'

Emanating from the success of their first restaurant, the Richters went on to set up two other raw, vegan restaurants in California. They were known as 'raw cafeterias' and became a meeting place for people seeking an alternative lifestyle. Mr and Mrs Richter did more than establish restaurants that could function 'without the aid of a cookstove'; Dr Richter gave weekly lectures to educate Americans on the benefits of a raw diet and Vera incorporated his ideas into her recipes.

Vera Richter adapted her restaurant's menu to create the world's first vegan raw cookbook, which she self-published in 1925, called *Mrs Richter's Cook-less Book.* This book is known to be the precursor to many modern day vegan cookbooks, and establishes Mrs Richter and her husband as amongst the first people to explore vegan and raw cooking. The Richters not only believed in wholesome eating, but in a wholesome lifestyle, in which you rejected the convoluted ways of the world, and lived in the most natural sense possible, sun gazing, barefoot walking, and wearing very little, to no clothing.

This idyllic lifestyle saw Dr and Mrs Richter up to their deaths, both living to the ages of 85 and 75 respectively. Their conviction in vegan and raw cooking is unparalleled, as they endeavoured against the odds and the norms of society, and brought healthier living to America, and the rest of the world.

The Philosophy of Uncooked Food

'Nature's food brings nature's mood;
Soul, mind, blood, are cleansed, made good.
Your outlook on life, disposition and moods,
Are brighter and happier when you eat natural foods.'
Vera Richter

Since we have discovered that as a nation we are scarcely more than fifty per cent efficient, there has been much study as to the cause and cure of such a deplorable condition. Drugs and stimulants have been tried and found wanting, for we have become steadily more deficient in the abounding health that was our birthright.

Now the attention of the thoughtful has turned to foods as being possibly the chief source of trouble, and after many years of careful study and experiments, experts are telling us that uncooked, or unfired, food is the answer to our problem, to have a sound mind in a sound body.

If we recognize the fact, first of all, that body, mind and spirit are absolutely interdependent, we have gone a long way toward understanding the necessity for correct feeding of the body that mind and spirit may develop.

Since the human body is composed of certain chemicals, accurately proportioned, and since food is intended for the replacement of worn-out body cells, it logically follows that the food must contain the correct chemicals, properly combined, for the purpose. We have had an era of improving upon nature until we can scarcely tell just what is left of the original food when it reaches our tables. Our wheat and rice have the most valuable parts polished off the exterior, and the corn has the oil and the heart removed from the interior, and we eat whatever the manufacturer has seen fit to leave for us. When nature manufactures a food for humans she puts into it the chemicals most needed and in the right proportions. There is much evidence that we should eat our food as nature has grown it, without adding to or subtracting from its original form, other than to remove the outer coverings that are not usually eaten.

The fact established, we turn to the change in the chemical combinations of food caused by cooking. Take, for instance, the iron so much in demand for making good red blood. Chemists tells us that spinach is rich in iron, so we proceed to cook the spinach, and by so doing completely change the chemistry of that vegetable until it is doubtful if it is even ordinarily wholesome. The fresh, crisp leaves were analyzed by the chemist, and not the sodden, bitter mass that we have when it is cooked. Under the process of cooking, the vitamins, so necessary to vigorous health, take wings and flee, and the life-giving properties of cooked food are greatly diminished thereby. It is estimated that a pound of uncooked food is equal in value to two pounds of cooked food. In addition, the body is hampered by the necessity for throwing off this large amount of waste.

'The tree of silence bears the fruit of peace.' *Arabian proverb*

We have no record of the time before foods were cooked, but it is an accepted fact that the human animal once ate his food fresh from nature's hands. It is also axiomatic that with so-called civilization we have departed from the simplicity of natural foods and have built up a bewilderingly complex system of feeding our bodies, until it would take a Philadelphia lawyer or an expert cook to tell just how many mixtures go into each of the dishes that appear upon our tables in the guise of daily bread.

One should understand that the adoption of an unfired diet does not mean a constant sacrifice of all the good 'eats' to which he has been accustomed. A taste for fresh and delicious fruits, vegetables, cereals and nuts is readily acquired, and a cleaner taste soon discovers a delicacy and sweetness in the unfired foods that the highly seasoned and cookery-disguised foods never had.

'Eat what nature produced for your food, and eat it as nature made it ready for you.'
Vera Richter

One is also sure that whatever he eats is fresh and inviting, for no decaying materials, no inferior ones, can be used when there is no cooking and seasoning to disguise the fact.

An alert, clear-headed, springy feeling is also the reward of the followers of nature's diet, and since one cannot readily over-eat, the super-abundant fat cells that make life a burden and induce disease should not be feared. If disease is already upon the consumer of fired foods, the way out is plain – eat what nature produced for your food, and eat it as nature made it ready for you. Unfired food does not produce disease, because it contains no inorganic sugar, soluble starch and partly decomposed protein; neither inorganic salts to irritate the nerves; nor does it readily decay and ferment in the alimentary canals and so produce toxic elements. It has true remedial value for curing disease by supplying the proper food elements in organic form.

Unfired food in proper combination, together with sunshine, fresh air, exercise and sleep, will promote and maintain health, physical, mental, moral and spiritual.

Preface

To the logical thinker it is plain that a sound body cannot be built of poor material. Of what does the right material for body-building consist? How shall we judge? We read many books, attend lectures, we hear diverse theories expounded.

We must judge by results. 'By their fruits ye shall know them.' A system of living which will take us through life without sickness and without fatigue is sought by all. Taking this as a criterion, the natural food system stands the test. It gets results—not only the negative results of freedom from sickness and fatigue, but creates a new feeling of wellbeing and vigor. However, those who have built their bodies year after year of poor material and too much of it, must not expect to rejuvenate themselves quickly. There are no miracles in Nature. Results of a lifetime of indulgence in cooked food cannot be expected to be eradicated by just a few meals of natural food.

People who have existed for years on devitalized food, when making the change to natural or uncooked food, sometimes complain of not feeling satisfied on their new diet. This is because their body cells are clamoring for the old stimulants, cooked foods, of which they are built.

Such individuals usually do not realize that the artificial energy which they experience for a time on the cooked food diet is but due to a whipping or irritation of the nerves by the poisons with which the system is loaded.

'There are no miracles in nature.' *Vera Richter*

In cleansing a dirty house dust will arise and inconveniences must be endured. When one resolves to cleanse the physical temple after a long period of wrong living it must be remembered that the eliminations which will occur are preliminaries in the rebuilding process. Perseverance must be the watchword during these temporary conditions, in the knowledge that the disagreeable symptoms will soon give way to normal and healthy reactions. It will be found that the cleansing period will be shortened if, in addition to natural food, sun and air baths are indulged in, thus encouraging elimination through the skin, also deep breathing and exercising. Remember that 'Nature cures,' and once the question of the proper care of the body is settled, the natural life may be lived automatically. It isn't necessary to talk and think food ad nauseam, but go about the real business of living, knowing that the body will not intrude upon our attention with the usual train of ills which mankind unnecessarily endures.

These recipes you will find simple, economical and satisfying to the unperverted taste—more so with time.

Vera Richter

- Dairy Fresh -

CARROT

Farm Fresh

FRESH PLANT
Guaranteed
100% Genuine

BEST IN TOWN

◆ Since 1972 ◆

Vegetable Salads

Shredded Carrots

Shred or grate eight medium carrots and serve with peanut dressing, French dressing or almond-banana dressing (see Dressings).

Red Cabbage Salad

Four cups finely chopped red cabbage, two cups minced endive, two cups chopped tomato. Mix thoroughly with eggless mayonnaise (see Dressings) and a squeeze of lemon. Serve on shredded lettuce.

Carrot-Celery-Onion Salad

Three stalks finely chopped celery, six medium carrots which have been put through food chopper (or processor),

a handful of finely minced parsley and a bunch of chopped spring onions. Mix with French dressing or eggless mayonnaise (see Dressings).

Carrot-Celery-Walnut Salad
Four stalks finely chopped celery, six medium carrots which have been run through food chopper (or processor) using medium-fine cutter, one cup finely chopped or ground walnut; mix well with eggless mayonnaise (see Dressings). This may be moulded in a shallow cup in individual portions and then emptied on a plate containing a lettuce leaf, garnishing each portion with whole walnuts.

Carrot-Endive Salad
Four cups endives chopped medium fine, six grated carrots, one-half cup flaked pine nuts. Mix well and drip over a little safflower oil or French dressing. (Editor's note: most truly raw oils are labeled 'cold' or 'expeller-pressed'—check with your retailer that your chosen variety is suitable for a raw diet.)

Celery-Olive Salad
Six stalks chopped celery, one cup shredded raw almonds and twenty pitted sun-dried olives. Chop the olives coarsely and mix with the celery and almonds,

moistening slightly with eggless mayonnaise (see Dressings) and thread over a little honey. Serve on lettuce leaf. (Editor's note: honey is not a vegan ingredient and it is not always raw. Thankfully nowadays, there's an array of modern alternatives to suit your dietary requirements, e.g. honey that has not been pasteurized; agave nectar—vegan, but not raw—date paste—both raw and vegan— and coconut nectar. Due to its relatively low glycemic index and syrupy consistency, I will be henceforth substituting coconut nectar for honey wherever Vera mentions it. Feel free to replace, however, with your own syrupy sweetener of choice.)

Stuffed Celery

Select eight stalks of celery with a deep curve. Fill with a mixture made as follows: into a bowl put four tablespoons of raw peanut butter, a handful of very finely minced parsley and two tablespoons tomato pulp. Mix well together. If liked, a little minced onion may be added.

Beansprout Salad

Four cups beansprouts, four stalks chopped celery, one cup chipped tomato, a bunch of minced spring onions. Mix well with French dressing. (Editor's note: by 'chipped tomato', Vera is almost certainly referring to dehydrated tomato chips. These are available to buy in stores, or can be made at home using a dehydrator—for those cooks who do not have regular access to the LA sunshine.)

Beet Salad

Put eight beets through food chopper, using medium-fine cutter. Dress with lemon-coconut nectar dressing (equal parts fresh lemon juice and coconut nectar beaten together). The flavor is improved by permitting the beets to blend with the dressing for an hour or so before serving.

Beet-Celery Salad

Four stalks chopped celery, four beets which have been put through food chopper, using fine cutter, one cup watercress tips which have been broken in small pieces. Mix with French dressing (see Dressings).

Onion Salad

Four cups sliced onions, two cups chopped watercress, two cups chipped tomatoes. Mix with French dressing.

Shredded Parsnips

Three shredded parsnips, two cups dried sweet corn which has been soaked several hours in just enough water to soften slightly. Don't soak in too much water or it will be mushy. These two flavors make a delicious blend. A little safflower oil may be dripped over, if liked.

Cabbage-Bell Pepper Salad

Half a medium cabbage chopped, two chopped bell peppers, a bunch of minced spring onions. Mix well and blend with French dressing. (Editor's note: this recipe will work with bell peppers of all colors, but red and green make for a lovely mix on the plate.)

Cabbage Combination Salad

Half a medium cabbage chopped or shredded, two cups each grated carrot, grated beet and minced celery, a handful of minced parsley and a bunch of chopped spring onions. Mix all ingredients well and blend with French dressing.

May's Salad

Half a medium cabbage chopped, two cups each of sliced radish and chipped tomato, a bunch of chopped spring onions, one chopped bell pepper (your color of choice) and a handful of minced parsley. Blend all ingredients well together and mix with French dressing or eggless mayonnaise. (Editor's note: by 'chipped tomato',

Vera is almost certainly referring to dehydrated tomato chips. Also see Dressings for the recipe for the eggless mayonnaise.)

Turnip-Olive Salad

Three tender turnips peeled and finely chopped, four chopped lettuce hearts (using the light-colored leaves), twenty pitted dried olives, minced. Mix well and drip over a very little safflower oil.

Spinach Salad

Shred six cups of well-washed and drained spinach leaves medium fine and dress with French dressing or raw peanut butter thinned with tomato juice. Two cups finely chopped mint leaves add a pleasing flavor.

Spinach-Watercress Salad

Three cups chopped spinach, three cups chopped watercress, a handful of minced parsley. Mix well with French dressing or eggless mayonnaise.

Spinach au naturel

Select six cups of tender spinach leaves. After cleansing and draining thoroughly, place in salad bowl with two cups sliced tomatoes. Moisten with French dressing and serve.

Lettuce-Celery Salad

Four cups of chopped lettuce, four stalks of celery and one chopped bell pepper. Mix together and drizzle with French dressing.

Combination Salad I

One medium lettuce chopped, two cups each of sliced radishes and chipped tomato, and a handful of minced parsley. Mix and drizzle with French dressing.

Combination Salad II

Chop one medium lettuce, three stalks of celery and one sweet green pepper. Mix with two cups chipped tomato. Flavor with a bunch of minced spring onions and drizzle with French dressing.

Asparagus Salad

Twenty asparagus tips, three cups each of watercress and sliced tomatoes. Place layers of asparagus and watercress in a salad bowl, then top with a layer of sliced tomatoes. Drizzle with French dressing and serve.

Green Peas

Tender green peas are delicious eaten right from the pod or shelled and mixed with almond-banana dressing. (See Dressings). (Editor's note: according to modern-day US government regulations, you'll want to allow half a cup—or 75g—per person. This counts as one serving of your recommended intake of vegetables.)

Corn au Naturel

In summer months, corn is delicious eaten straight from the cob au naturel. Select eight ears of tender corn and slice from cob. Add a handful of minced parsley and a bunch of minced spring onions. Mix with eggless mayonnaise and serve on lettuce leaf.

Irish Potato Salad

Four medium potatoes—peeled, sliced, and chopped— one-half cup cabbage chopped, one-half cup raw peanuts or pine nuts, a handful of minced parsley and four chopped spring onions. Mix well and drizzle with a tablespoonful of your favorite oil.

Potato Medley

Slice fine two potatoes (either Irish or sweet), one small turnip, a carrot, two small onions and a cucumber. Add a finely grated beet and a handful of minced parsley. Mix with a little French dressing and serve on lettuce leaf.

Sorrel Salad

Four cups chopped sheep sorrel or English sorrel, two cups chopped watercress. Mix well and drizzle with a teaspoonful of your cold-pressed oil of choice. No lemon juice need be used with this, since the sorrel itself supplies a tantalizingly tart taste. (Editor's note: Mrs Richter was a great believer in the healing powers of sorrel and this leafy, spinach-like vegetable is indeed rich in vitamins A, B6 and C, as well as various antioxidant compounds.)

Stuffed Peppers

Select four sweet bell peppers, as nearly round shaped as possible. Cut out stem end and remove center. Fill with chopped cabbage mixed with eggless mayonnaise and a little minced spring onion, if you like. Serve on lettuce leaf. (Editor's note: though Vera doesn't specify a particular color, riper red or yellow peppers will give a much sweeter, smokier flavor than their green counterparts.)

Pepper Salad

Mince finely four small green peppers and two small sweet red peppers. Mix with three tablespoons of finely chopped onion and the same amount of minced parsley. Blend with French dressing.

Spanish Relish

Thinly slice one medium cucumber and mix with two chopped

bell peppers, two large tomatoes cut into small chips, and one minced onion. A few minced nasturtium leaves or chopped green nasturtium seed pods will add a piquant peppery flavor. If nasturtiums are not available, a tablespoon of grated horseradish will have the same effect. These ingredients are all juicy and dramatic, and very little dressing, if any, is required.

Tonic Salad
Run three turnips, six carrots and four beets through food chopper. Add four stalks of chopped celery, half a cup of flaked pine nuts and mix well together. Drip over a tablespoon of oil, mix again and serve.

Artichoke Salad
Put one pound of well-scrubbed, well-drained Jerusalem artichokes through food chopper, using medium-fine cutter. To this, add half a cup each of minced spring onions, parsley and raw peanuts. Mix well and drizzle with a tablespoonful of oil.

Vegetable Loaf
Six carrots and two beef tomatoes which have been put through food chopper using fine cutter, four stalks finely chopped celery, a handful of minced parsley, three tablespoons of oil and two cloves of garlic which have been very finely minced and crushed. Stir in pine nuts or raw pistachio nuts until the mixture is stiff enough to

mould. Mix all ingredients well together then pour into oblong loaf pan which has been moistened slightly with oil. Empty the loaf onto a platter and garnish with parsley. Raw peanut butter dressing goes well with this. Many variations of flavor are possible with this dish, substituting sage or thyme, savory, etc., for the parsley. (Editor's note: in Vera's experience, using pistachios instead of pine nuts gives the loaf an entirely different flavor.)

Radish Salad
Slice crisp, fresh radishes and mix with half as much sliced spring onions. Drizzle with French dressing. (Editor's note: allow approximately one cup per person for a delicious side salad.)

Radish Roses
Select round red radishes for this purpose; scrub well but do not scrape. Begin at the root end and make six incisions through skin running three-fourths length of the radish. Pass knife under the sections of skin and cut down as far as incisions extend. Place in cold water before serving and the sections of skin will fold

back, giving the radish a flower-like appearance. (Editor's note: Vera's roses make a stunning garnish to any dish, adding instant glamour to your plate.)

Beauty Salad I

Asparagus (tender tips only) eaten freely with mint sauce (see Dressings). (Editor's note: Vera was a firm believer in the benefits of this deliciously fresh green combination. She wrote of how it 'will induce light perspiration, aiding circulation and clearing the complexion'. Though it's unlikely to raise your temperature, asparagus is loaded with vitamins and antioxidants—making it a delicious way to battle the aging process.)

Beauty Salad II

Eight stalks chopped celery, three cups of chopped onion, using either spring onions or a mild Spanish variety. Drizzle with French dressing, mix well and serve.

Brazilian Salad

One pineapple peeled and grated, four stalks chopped celery, half a cup of chopped Brazil nuts. Blend the ingredients and serve on sprays of parsley, drizzled with a little coconut nectar. (Editor's

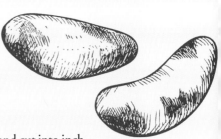

note: to keep this recipe raw and/or vegan, please ensure you shop for raw Brazil nuts.)

Tomato Sandwich

Select four large firm tomatoes and cut into inch-thick slices. Mince finely equal parts of watercress, parsley and spring onion, mix well with eggless mayonnaise (editor's note: quantities will vary depending on how much 'filling' you want your sandwiches to have) and spread onto tomato slices. Serve on lettuce leaf and garnish with an extra sprinkling of parsley.

Stuffed Tomatoes

Select four well-shaped, firm tomatoes and, cutting out stem end, scoop out the center. Mince finely three stalks of celery, a handful of parsley and four spring onions to flavor. Mix well with eggless mayonnaise and fill tomatoes with this mixture (see Dressings). Garnish with an extra sprinkling of parsley.

Tomato and Cucumber Salad

Arrange alternate slices of tomato and cucumber until six slices have been piled one on top of the other. Serve on lettuce leaves and garnish with strips of red and green peppers. French dressing or eggless mayonnaise may be used with this. (Editor's note: Vera's vegetable stacks make for a colorful alternative to more conventional finger foods—perfect for health-conscious dinner guests! Also, see Dressings for mayonnaise and French dressing recipes.)

Sliced Tomatoes

Slice six well-shaped tomatoes in one-third-inch slices and arrange on lettuce leaves. A few finely chopped chives may be sprinkled over the tomatoes, or a tablespoonful of finely chopped cucumber placed on the center of each slice. Serve with French dressing.

Summer Salad

Two stalks of chopped celery, two handfuls of string beans sliced very thin, two summer squashes (also known as yellow courgettes) cut into small dice and two carrots which have been run through food chopper. These vegetables should be tender. Sprinkle with a tablespoonful of fresh lemon juice and two tablespoons chopped spring onion. Mix all the vegetables together with eggless mayonnaise, allowing them to blend for half an hour before serving.

Cauliflower Salad

One small cauliflower chopped medium fine, two chopped bell peppers, one cup of chopped watercress and six spring onions to flavor. Mix with eggless mayonnaise.

Green Peas and Carrot

Put three cups of green peas and six carrots through food chopper. A few chopped mint leaves added give a pleasing flavor. Mix with almond-banana dressing.

Cucumber Salad

Peel two large cucumbers, cut in half lengthwise, scoop out the seeds, then cut in long, thin strips. Marinate in French dressing in a cool place for half an hour, drain and serve on lettuce leaves, garnishing with chopped parsley.

Carrot-Pineapple Salad

Two chopped carrots, one peeled and shredded pineapple, one small onion chopped. Mix with eggless mayonnaise (see Dressings) and serve on lettuce leaf.

Cabbage-Coconut Salad

Half a cabbage shredded, one medium cucumber diced, two stalks celery chopped, one cup shredded coconut. Mix with eggless mayonnaise (see Dressings) and serve on lettuce leaf.

Turnip-Carrot Salad

Run four turnips and seven carrots through a food

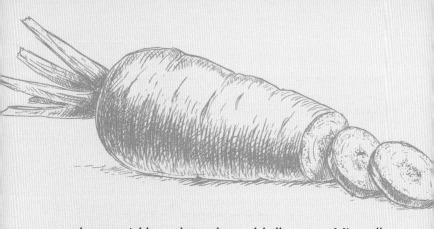

chopper. Add one large chopped bell pepper. Mix well and pour over French dressing.

Waldorf Salad

Mix lightly two cups diced apple, one cup chopped celery, one-half cup chopped walnuts or pecans, one-half cup seedless sun-dried raisins. Mix with eggless mayonnaise and serve on lettuce leaf, garnishing each portion with whole walnuts. Drizzle with a little coconut nectar if you like.

Nut Roll

String eight stalks of celery, removing all fiber; run through food chopper and press out the juice. To two cups of this ground celery add one cup flaked pine nuts, two tablespoons mashed avocado, two tablespoons very finely minced spring onion, two tablespoons minced parsley and one tablespoon eggless mayonnaise. Flavor with powdered garlic and powdered sage. Very thoroughly mix and blend all ingredients, form into a roll and wrap in baking paper moistened with eggless mayonnaise. Slice, serve on lettuce leaf with slice of mild onion, radish and a sprig of parsley.

Sandwich Fillings

Date, Fig and Nut

One-half cup dried figs, one cup pitted sun-dried dates, one-half cup nuts, one-half cup orange juice, one tablespoon fresh lemon juice. Put figs, dates and nuts through food chopper. Mix thoroughly with orange and fresh lemon juice, and spread. (Editor's note: versatile Vera doesn't often insist on a particular kind of nut and so feel free to experiment with your favorite raw varieties, from satisfyingly chunky walnuts to delicious pistachio rubble. Also, rather than trawling the aisles of your local supermarket for raw, unpasteurized fruit juices, why not try squeezing your own?)

Olive and Nut

One cup raw nuts (of your choice), one-half cup pitted sundried olives, one-half cup eggless mayonnaise (see

Dressings). Chop nuts and olives finely, mix thoroughly with mayonnaise, and spread.

Raisin

Two cups seedless raisins, one-half cup eggless mayonnaise. Put the raisins through food chopper. Add the eggless mayonnaise gradually, mix thoroughly, and spread.

Raisin and Nut

One cup seedless raisins, one cup nuts. Run through food chopper, then mix thoroughly with a tablespoon of fresh grape juice until spreadable. (Editor's note: if you're struggling to find unpasteurized grape juice in the shops, it's easy to make your own at home. Simply mix two to three cups of grapes with a dash of water in a blender. Strain out the solids and your juice will be ready to serve.)

Carrot-Celery

Grind up three carrots and two stalks of celery in a food chopper until you've produced a fine mix. Add two-thirds as much finely ground raw nuts (walnuts are particularly good with this). Flavor with a handful of finely minced onion, mix with eggless mayonnaise dressing, and spread.

Cucumber-Celery

Half a cucumber and two stalks of celery, chopped fine, a pinch of minced onion for flavoring, and one half-cup chopped nuts. Moisten with eggless mayonnaise dressing. Put crisp lettuce leaf on each slice of bread before spreading with this mixture.

Green Pepper

Chop finely one sweet green pepper, moisten with mayonnaise, and spread.

Nut-Rich Nectar

Two tablespoons unroasted peanut butter mixed with coconut nectar to a spreadable consistency. Proportion of coconut nectar used depends upon the consistency of the peanut butter. If stiff, more coconut nectar is needed; oily peanut butter requires less.

Avocado

Peel a fully ripe avocado, cut into halves and mash with a fork until smooth and spreadable. Season with a pinch of celery salt or powdered garlic.

Fruit Salads

Fruit Medley

One apple peeled and cubed, two bananas, one orange and one pineapple cut into chunks. To add a touch of color, finish with a dusting of pomegranate seeds or a spoonful of finely minced cranberries that have been sweetened with coconut nectar.

Fruit Salad

Half a pound of strawberries halved, two bananas cubed, and half a pound of cherries pitted and halved. Drizzle with coconut nectar and mix with two handfuls of grated pineapple, grated coconut or finely chopped raw almonds. This recipe can be varied or changed according to the fruits and berries in season.

Cinnamon Apple Shreds

Grate up five apples. Stir in several heaped tablespoons of

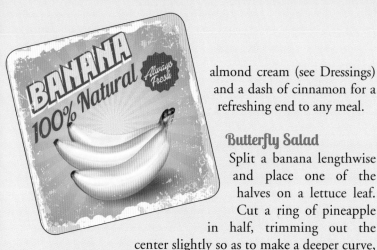

almond cream (see Dressings) and a dash of cinnamon for a refreshing end to any meal.

Butterfly Salad

Split a banana lengthwise and place one of the halves on a lettuce leaf. Cut a ring of pineapple in half, trimming out the center slightly so as to make a deeper curve, and place one of these half-slices of pineapple on each side of the banana piece, having the outside edges of the pineapple half next the banana. Peel a grapefruit and cut therefrom a thin slice crosswise. Cut the slice in half and trim out the center where the seeds grow with a knife, making a curve. Place these grapefruit slices on top of the two pineapple pieces. Over these, place slices of orange prepared like the grapefruit. Garnish the orange slices with spots of finely minced or ground pistachio nuts and pomegranate seeds. From a peeled banana take, with a small scoop, a round piece for the butterfly's head. The antennae may be made from tiny slivers of green pepper.

Banana-Peanut Salad

One cup shelled unroasted peanuts, four large fully ripe bananas, a handful of white grapes and eggless mayonnaise dressing. Put peanuts through food chopper, using medium-fine cutter, split bananas and roll them in mayonnaise dressing, then in the chopped peanuts. Serve on lettuce leaves, using white grapes for garnish.

Pineapple-Banana Salad

From a firm head of lettuce cut a slice about half an inch thick. On top of this place a slice of pineapple and on this banana cut in long strips. Top with mayonnaise dressing sprinkled with chopped nuts and garnish plate with pecan halves.

Pineapple-Celery Salad

One fully ripe pineapple diced, six stalks of finely chopped celery and two handfuls of seedless sun-dried raisins. Eggless mayonnaise dressing may be mixed with this or a coconut nectar drizzled over, as preferred. Leave to sit for half an hour before serving.

Orange Rose

Select four well-shaped, thin-skinned oranges (editor's note: today's easy-peel varieties are perfect for this recipe). Peel them, carefully removing as much of the tough white membrane as possible without mangling the pulp. Now separate the inner segments, opening them up almost all the way to give the effect of a budding rose. Fill in the center and the space between the 'petals' with vibrant orange persimmon (sharon fruit) pulp.

Orange-Pineapple Salad

Select a fully ripe pineapple. Peel, remove eyes, cut into dice and mix with four diced oranges and half a cup of finely chopped almonds.

Orange Baskets

Select four large oranges with smooth skins and a high round shape. Score a handle, about half an inch wide, across the top hemisphere of the orange. Cut below the handle on each side, all the way down to the 'equator' of the orange, removing peel and pulp as you go. Using a paring knife and spoon, continue to scoop out pulp from under the handle and inside the basket. Fill the hollowed-out basket with grapes or chopped bananas and raw nuts.

Orange-Mint Salad

Cut four large oranges in half crosswise and set about scooping out pulp with a spoon, rejecting membrane and seeds as you go. To the sweet and juicy pulp, add two tablespoons of finely chopped mint, two tablespoons of coconut nectar and two teaspoons of freshly squeezed lemon juice. Serve in your prettiest sherbet glasses and garnish each with a sprig of mint. (Editor's note: this recipe calls for a set of sherbet glasses. With its long, elegant stem, the sherbet glass

will help you serve up a
show-stopping dessert
every time.)

Tangerine Salad

Peel and separate four
tangerines into sections.
To this, add half a fresh
pineapple shredded and three
diced bananas. Mix well and drip
over a little coconut nectar.

Cranberry Relish

Pick over and wash cranberries. Put three cups through
food chopper, using medium-fine cutter. Mash and mix
in four fully ripe bananas, sweeten with coconut nectar
and beat well. The flavor is improved by permitting it to
blend for an hour or so before serving.

Formula I

Two peeled and diced pears, two oranges peeled and split
into segments, and one cup red grapes cut into halves.
Mix with half a cup of chopped raw walnuts or pine nuts.

Formula II

One cup of finely chopped, sun-dried figs, half cups of pitted
dates and prunes, also chopped. Mix with a small quantity
of carob meal. (Editor's note: today, carob can be purchased

in an array of different forms. For this recipe, organic carob chips add a delicious hit of sweetness and crunch—great news for anyone suffering from chocolate cravings.)

Formula 111
Mix one cup of white grapes with equal quantities of strawberries, raspberries, cubed bananas, oranges, and pineapple. Finish with a generous drizzle of coconut nectar.

Peach Salad 1
Mix four sliced peaches with four sliced bananas. Arrange on a lettuce leaf and pour over almond cream. (See Dressings).

Peach Salad 11
Peel and halve a fine ripe peach (editor's note: one peach per dinner guest), place on a lettuce leaf and sprinkle generously with chopped raw almonds. Drizzle with a little coconut nectar and serve.

Cherry-Nut Salad
Carefully remove the pits from a bag or a box of perfectly ripe, large cherries. In the meantime have an equal number of hazelnuts marinating in French dressing. When ready to serve, stuff each cherry

with a nut in place of the pit. Serve up two to three heaped tablespoons on a nest of fresh green lettuce.

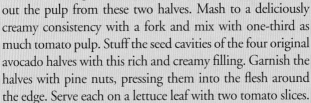

Avocado Salad

Cut in half lengthwise two ripe but firm avocados; remove seeds. Repeat with a third avocado. Using a teaspoon, scoop out the pulp from these two halves. Mash to a deliciously creamy consistency with a fork and mix with one-third as much tomato pulp. Stuff the seed cavities of the four original avocado halves with this rich and creamy filling. Garnish the halves with pine nuts, pressing them into the flesh around the edge. Serve each on a lettuce leaf with two tomato slices.

Avocado-Orange Salad

Peel and pit four perfectly ripe avocado pears. Slice thinly and combine with segments from two large oranges. For each serving, arrange the fruit slices on a lettuce leaf in pleasing, multicolored circles.

Avocado Cocktail

For two people: cut medium-sized avocado in half, remove stone, peel and cut the pulp in small cubes. Sprinkle lightly with a fresh lemon juice and leave to stand in a

cool place for half an hour. Peel and dice an orange in small pieces the same size as the avocado cubes. Mix lightly together with three tablespoons of freshly squeezed orange juice and a teaspoon of coconut nectar, and serve in your favorite glasses.

Prune Whip

Wash well and soak one-and-a-half cups of raw, pitted prunes in water until thoroughly soft. Drain and put through food chopper, then through colander. Stir in half a cup of pine nuts and beat well together with a rotary beater. Drizzle in a little coconut nectar to taste.

Date Butter

Mash one cup dates (the dark, small, seeded variety are best for this) or they can be run through food chopper, then pour over two tablespoons of warm water and beat to a pulp. Add eight tablespoons unroasted peanut butter and blend well with mashed dates. This is a very satisfying spread for sun-dried wafers, or may be spread on split bananas.

Nature's Nectar

Don't spoil your sun-dried peaches, figs, apricots, pears, etc., by cooking them. It isn't necessary. Wash well and soak overnight in cool water. The water in which the fruits are soaked makes for a refreshing drink.

Summer Fruit Salad
Peel and slice three peaches and three pears, then add one-half cup diced pineapple and one-half cup diced watermelon. Thread over a little coconut nectar and set aside to blend in a cool place for half an hour.

Fruit Cup
Equal parts peeled and diced peaches, seedless grapes, and raspberries. Mix with a little coconut nectar and serve in sherbet glasses.

Avocado Fruit Salad
Slice up two avocados (peeled and pitted), three apples and five Japanese persimmons, and mix well. Arrange each portion on a fresh, green lettuce leaf.

Orange-Date Cocktail
Peel four oranges, remove the white, fibrous skin, then mince in small pieces. Add a cup of dates, cut very small, and a cup of shredded coconut. Add a little coconut nectar, if you like it, and mix well.

Grapefruit with Cranberries

Peel a grapefruit; carefully remove the skin around the sections. Arrange in a circle on a crisp lettuce leaf. Fill the center with cranberry relish (recipe given).

Porcupine Salad

Remove the peel from a large ripe pear. Cut in half and remove core. Now lay one half, flat side down, on salad plate containing lettuce leaf and insert almonds that you have cut into slivers. Use as many slivers as densely as you can to achieve the full porcupine effect. If you are inclined to decorate, you can make a little face on the pear with a bit of bell pepper, cranberry or whatever you have handy in the way of fruit.

Favorite Salad

Peel twelve tangerines, remove membrane, cut coarsely. Add two chopped sweet peppers and two stalks of celery. Sprinkle with half a cup of freshly squeezed grapefruit juice. Set aside to blend in a cool place for half an hour, drain and serve on lettuce leaf with mayonnaise dressing.

Avocado Cocktail

Peel and pit two avocados, cut into dice, then moisten with a dressing composed of two tablespoons strained tomato juice

and one tablespoon freshly
squeezed lemon juice. Equal
parts of avocado and celery
(diced) may be used, if
preferred. Put in cool place
to blend for half an hour before serving.

Persimmon Relish

Peel a box or a bag of persimmons. Crush with fork
until persimmon pulp is of smooth consistency. For
each dinner guest, fill a cocktail glass three-quarters of
the way with persimmon pulp. Then cut a two-inch
piece from the tip of a banana and separate (lengthwise)
into four equal parts. Put these four banana sticks into
the persimmon pulp, at the edge of the glass, at equal
distances. Fill center with powdered pecans, and top with
a whole pecan.

PREMIUM
Organic
PRODUCT

100% NATURAL

Orange Juice

- LOCALLY GROWN -

Dressings

French Dressing (as made at the Eutropheon)

Three tablespoons corn or safflower oil, one tablespoon freshly squeezed and strained lemon juice, one teaspoonful of coconut nectar. Beat well together.

Mint Sauce

Wash a generous bunch of mint and strip the leaves from the stems, patting them dry between clean cloths. Chop very fine, then measure. For each three tablespoons of mint, add two tablespoons of coconut nectar. Mix well, put in glass, cover and leave to stand in the sunshine for several hours. The coconut nectar draws out the flavor of the mint. Then add one-half cup of freshly squeezed lemon juice.

Eggless Mayonnaise

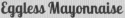

Place a ripe banana in a bowl and mash with a fork until perfectly smooth and free from lumps. Now stir in oil, a small quantity at a time, beating constantly with a rotary motion. Add fresh lemon juice to taste and more oil, stirring steadily until thickened. The mayonnaise may be colored green or pink as desired by mincing parsley finely and rubbing to a paste with a spoon and adding to the dressing after it is made, or by stirring in a little strained strawberry, raspberry, or beet juice. (Editor's note: since the Eutropheon first opened its doors, many new ingredients and products have come onto the market, making it easier for vegans to substitute their favorite dairy/egg-based ingredients. Not only is vegan mayonnaise available to buy readymade, you can also use unsweetened soy milk as a base for you to make your own. One-half cup soy milk combined with one cup groundnut oil, two teaspoons of cider vinegar and just a pinch of sea salt, and run through a blender, will give a silky approximation of egg-based mayo.)

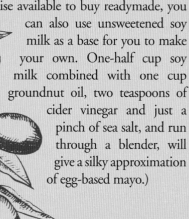

Sesame Seed Dressing

To your salad of choice, add a squeeze of lemon and a pinch of vegetable powder to season (editor's note: from spinach to spirulina, vegetable powders are a fantastic way to add instant nutritional content to your dishes). Then sprinkle on as many sesame seeds as you'd desire, adding subtle crunch to your salad. Toss and mix thoroughly, leave to sit for four or five minutes; toss and mix again. The absence of extracted oil will not be missed; sesame seeds have high oil content and will make a very satisfying salad.

Almond-Banana Dressing

Mash a ripe banana with a fork until creamy and smooth (editor's note: eliminate the last few lumps with a modern mini-chopper), add the same amount of almond butter and thin with half as much cool water. When well beaten add two tablespoons of eggless mayonnaise and teaspoonful coconut nectar and beat again.

Almond Cream

One tablespoon almond butter, two tablespoons cool water. Work the water into the almond butter, add teaspoonful coconut nectar and beat until creamy.

Orange-Cream Dressing

Three tablespoons orange juice, one tablespoon flaked pine nuts. Beat

together until creamy, then set aside to blend for an hour, when it will be ready to use after stirring thoroughly.

Rhubarb Dressing

Homemade rhubarb juice (made by blending stalks and straining out solids) drizzled over any vegetable salad is wholesome and refreshing, or if preferred, mix four tablespoons rhubarb juice with one tablespoon of flaked peanuts or pine nuts and set aside to blend for ten minutes.

Simplicity Dressing

Into a cold bowl put three tablespoons of olive or corn oil, two tablespoons of fresh lemon juice and one tablespoon each of onion juice and finely minced parsley. A dash of paprika will add heat. Beat well and prepare to douse your salad therewith. (Editor's note: onion juice can easily be obtained by grating or grinding a whole, peeled onion in a blender and then straining out the solids.)

Tomato-Peanut Dressing

Two tablespoons unroasted peanut butter, three tablespoons tomato juice and two tablespoons safflower oil. Work the tomato juice into the peanut butter and add the oil, beating until perfectly smooth.

Peanut Butter Dressing

One tablespoon of unroasted peanut butter, four tablespoons cool water and one of freshly squeezed lemon juice. Put the peanut butter in a bowl and add the fluids gradually, stirring constantly to prevent lumpiness and ensure you get a smooth, creamy consistency. A tablespoon each of very finely minced parsley and onion improves this recipe.

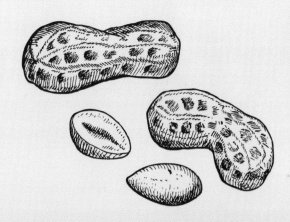

PREMIUM QUALITY

Farm Fresh

Tomato

100% NATURAL

PREMIUM
★★★
Organic
PRODUCT

Soups

Avocado Soup

Put twelve whole tomatoes through food chopper and strain through coarse colander. Mix three cups strained tomato juice and pulp, two cups avocado pulp (obtained by mashing peeled avocado with fork) and one-half cup flaked pine nuts. Stir (editor's note: or perhaps blend), all together well, until creamy.

Fruit Soup

One tablespoon almond butter, five tablespoons freshly squeezed orange juice, two tablespoons cool water. Add the orange juice and water to the almond butter gradually, removing all lumps and beating until smooth and creamy, then add one large banana that you have peeled and mashed with a fork until liquid. Beat all these ingredients thoroughly together and this will form the body of the soup (one serving). Two tablespoons of pineapple cut

into very small cubes may now be added, or the same amount of fully ripe strawberries, cut in half. Red raspberries, mashed with a fork, may be used instead of the strawberries. If these fruits are not available two tablespoons of cranberry relish (see Fruit Salads) may be substituted, stirring thoroughly into the body of the soup.

Cereal Soup

Soak half a pound of oatmeal in warm water for several hours, or overnight, then put through a sieve, and to the cream thus obtained add one cup each of strained tomato juice and pulp, and finely ground celery. Flavor with three tablespoons finely minced parsley and two tablespoons grated onion, or a clove of very finely minced and crushed garlic instead of the onion, as preferred. This soup may be varied by substituting the pulp of tender corn, scraped from the cob, for the celery, or the juice and pulp of grated cucumbers.

Tomato Cream Soup

Put tomatoes and celery through food chopper, proportion being three cups tomato pulp to one cup each celery and peanut butter. Put the ground tomato pulp and celery through sieve, then add peanut butter, creaming it into the liquid until smooth and without lumps. Now add two tablespoons parsley and one large clove of garlic, very finely minced, two tablespoons of oil, and beat all ingredients well together.

Onion Soup

Grind or grate fine two onions and press out all the juice using a strainer. Add the juice to two cups of tomato juice, two tablespoons of pine nuts and a tablespoon minced parsley. Allow to sit and blend for half an hour before serving.

Beverages

Fruit Punch

Crush one quart of strawberries to a pulp. Add three cups fresh grape juice or bananas mashed with a fork, two cups orange juice and five cups cold water. Sweeten to taste with coconut nectar and stir well. When you are ready to serve, halve a handful of strawberries and float in your drink.

Fruit Nectar

May be obtained by pressing the juice from blackberries, raspberries, strawberries, grapes, fully ripe pitted apricots, etc. Strain the juice and dilute to taste with chilled water. A little coconut nectar may be added as desired. A small fruit press will be found convenient for extracting the juice.

Rhubarb Tonic Drink

Four tablespoons homemade rhubarb juice, an equal amount of cold water, one teaspoon beet juice (this will

give it a pretty pink color), one teaspoon coconut nectar. Stir well and serve. Rhubarb juice may be obtained by grating rhubarb stalks or putting them through juice extractor.

Lemonade

Put into eight-ounce glass three teaspoons strained lemon juice and one teaspoonful coconut nectar. Fill the glass with cold water, stir well and serve.

Orangeade

Fill a drinking glass one-quarter full of freshly squeezed orange juice, add a teaspoon of coconut nectar, fill up glass with cold water, stir well and serve.

Herbade

Soak in a cup of water for one or two hours a teaspoonful of sun-dried beet tops, celery tops, mint or similar herbs. Strain through sieve, stir into it a teaspoon of coconut nectar and serve. Where beet tops are used, substitute a teaspoon of freshly squeezed lemon juice for coconut nectar.

Almond Milk

One tablespoon almond butter, five tablespoons cool water, one teaspoon coconut nectar. Add the water to the almond butter gradually, stirring well to remove lumps, then add coconut nectar, beating until smooth and frothy.

Carob Drink
A teaspoonful of carob meal added to almond milk prepared as above gives a delicious flavor and is very nutritious.

Tomato Tonic Drink
One-half glass strained tomato juice. Fill up the glass with cold water, stir well and serve. A few crushed mint leaves, or a teaspoonful of fresh lemon juice or coconut nectar added to this may improve it for some.

Fabulous Fiber Drink

Stir one cup of whole flaxseed into eight cups (2 litres) of cold water. Shake thoroughly several times and leave to stand over night. Strain the seeds from the water. Enriched with nutrients, this water is ready to drink and can be sipped throughout the day. Add fresh water to the seeds, stir a few times and leave to stand until the following morning; the water that is strained from this being your drink throughout the next day. Repeat the process to provide drinking water for a third day. The flaxseed may also be eaten as a nutritious snack.

Mint Cocktail

Extract the juice of five oranges, two lemons and one grapefruit. Strain through sieve and put in a large pitcher,

adding three quarters of a cup of coconut nectar, a small handful of crushed mint leaves and half a banana, sliced. Dilute to taste with ice-cold water.

If at any time we are costive, there is no medicine better than some sort of food which will purge you gently and with ease, the trial of which is familiar to all, and the use without any pain.

PREMIUM QUALITY
PREMIUM
Organic
PRODUCT
Legendary
Grapes
100% NATURAL

Sun–Dried Breads

Carob Bread

Run two pounds pitted dates and one pound seedless raisins through chopper, and work into it as much finely ground carob as it will hold. It should be sufficiently stiff to roll out. Cut into wafers of half-inch thickness and expose to the sunshine for several hours to dry slightly. (Editor's note: since her café, the Eutropheon, was based in LA, sunshine was never in short supply for Vera Richter. If you're not lucky enough to be living in such a clement climate, dehydrators provide a modern-day shortcut to Vera's sun-dried perfection, allowing you to create beautiful unfired pies, breads and vegetable chips without even leaving the comfort of your kitchen!)

Nut Bread

Grind coarsely one-half cup almonds, one tablespoon walnuts, two tablespoons pine nuts. Add one-half cup

flaked oats (or wheat or rice), mix all thoroughly and moisten with water. Spread in a thin layer. Sprinkle the top with carob chips and expose to the sunshine for at least an hour.

Raisin-Nut Bread

Three pounds raisins, one-half pound almonds, one-half pound wheat meal. Mix and put through processor. If not sufficiently stiff to roll out, work in more wheat meal, roll thin and cut into wafers. If desired, whole flaxseed may be sprinkled on the board on which the mass is rolled out and it will adhere. Expose to the sunshine for several hours to dry slightly.

Whole-Wheat Bread

Wash and soak four pounds of recleaned wheat overnight in cold water. In the morning put in a sack and hang up to drain for an hour or so, then put through wheat grinder (editor's note: if you don't have a wheat grinder, whole-wheat flour is now available to buy in most stores). Now mix in a pint of corn oil, adding enough cool water to thin sufficiently to roll out. Sprinkle wheat meal on the board on which you roll out to prevent sticking, cut into wafers, then expose to the sunshine until thoroughly dry.

Energizing Flaxseed Loaf

One pound whole wheat meal, ten oz. whole flaxseed, three oz. almonds, six oz. raisins, half-cup corn oil, half-cup coconut nectar. Break up the almonds coarsely by running them through food chopper. Put the wheat meal in a bowl, add the flaxseed, almonds and raisins, and mix all well together. Make a little hollow in the center of the dough, pour in oil and coconut nectar and mix thoroughly again. (Editor's note: loaded with fiber and slow-releasing carbohydrates, Vera's flaxseed loaf is perfect for whenever you're in need of a little extra energy).

Banana Wafers

One cup coarsely ground wheat, one-half cup each finely chopped figs and prunes and two mashed-up bananas. Blend all these ingredients together and then add one-half cup coconut nectar. Mix again. Roll out into layers of one-quarter inch thickness. Slice into narrow wafers and leave in the sunshine to dry.

Flaked Oats with Raisins

One cup flaked or rolled oats, one-half cup each seedless raisins and shredded coconut. Mix thoroughly into the oats. Drizzle with coconut nectar and/or almond milk for a delicious breakfast. (Editor's note: although shop-bought almond milk is not raw, you can make your own at home without the need for pasteurization. Simply soak almonds in water overnight. Place one cup almonds and three cups of water in a blender. Mix thoroughly and strain off the milk.)

Everyday Bread

One cup whole wheat, one-half cup unroasted peanuts and one-fourth cup pitted dried prunes. Grind the whole wheat coarsely, then the peanuts and mix into the wheat. Now grind the prunes and mix the three ingredients well together. Eaten dry, this bread will help promote healthy digestion every day. (Editor's note: at the time of writing, little was known about celiac disease and/or various other gluten intolerances that sufferers can develop at various times in their lives. This recipe is most definitely not recommended for anyone suffering from a similar food allergy!)

Tamales

Two cups of corn meal made from dried sweet corn; flavor with chili powder, a pinch of raw cumin seeds and two cloves crushed garlic. Mix well then stir in tomato or celery juice and cold-pressed olive oil, moistening enough so that the resulting dough is of the right consistency to be formed into tamale shape.

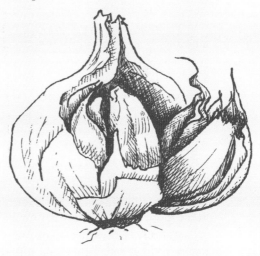

PREMIUM
Organic
PRODUCT

Sweet
Grapes
- LOCALLY GROWN -

Cakes

Fruit Cake

1 lb. pitted dates, 1 lb. seedless raisins, 4 oz. dried peaches, 4 oz. dried bananas, 8 oz. almonds. Cut the dried bananas in inch pieces, mix all ingredients thoroughly and run through food chopper. Press the mass firmly into a cake ring, set aside to harden for an hour or so, when it may be emptied on a plate and sliced. (Editor's note: Vera doesn't specify a particular size of cake pan/cake ring, but a standard eight-inch affair should suffice for most of the recipes in this section.)

Layer Cake

1 lb. dried black figs, 1 lb. seeded dates, 1 lb. coconut-nectar mixture, made by working into coconut nectar as much shredded coconut as it will hold. Put figs and dates through food chopper separately. Slightly moisten

with corn oil an oblong cake pan and press into it firmly pound of black figs, smooth over the top with a spoon. Then add the coconut nectar mixture, spreading evenly over the fig layer, and lastly the pound of chopped dates. To finish, press the three layers firmly together and smooth the top. In an hour or less the cake may be emptied onto a plate or your prettiest stand. Sprinkle with shredded coconut and a few walnuts or pecans and keep in a cool place until the next day, when it will be ready to slice.

Edible Almond Hearts

1/2 lb. rice flour, 1/2 lb. almond butter, 1 lb. pitted dates that have been run through food chopper. Put rice flour into a mixing bowl and work into it the almond butter. When well blended add pitted dates and thoroughly knead all ingredients together. This may be pressed into a single cake ring or else rolled out in a thin layer. Using a heart-shaped cookie cutter, create many smaller individual cakes, pressing a whole almond into the center of each to finish.

Carob Fruit Cake

1 lb. pitted dates, 10 oz. seedless raisins, 7 oz. figs, 5 oz. almonds, 10 oz. finely ground carob powder. Chop figs in small pieces, mix all ingredients thoroughly together and

put through food chopper. Firmly press the mixture into an eight-inch cake ring to mould. In an hour or less empty onto a serving plate and dust with shredded coconut.

Fruit-Nut Cake

1 lb. pitted dates, 1 lb. white figs (editor's note: also sold as 'Adriatic' or 'candy-striped' figs), 1 lb. seedless raisins, 1 lb. English walnuts, 1 lb. shredded coconut. Cut the figs in pieces and run all ingredients through food chopper. Mix thoroughly and press firmly into cake ring. In several hours it may be emptied onto a platter and sliced.

Elizabeth's Cake

1/2 lb. pitted dates, 1/2 lb. coconut nectar mixture (see Layer Cake recipe for details of how to make this ingredient), 1/4 lb. flaked pine nuts, 2 medium size oranges, 6 medium size apples, 1 unfired pie crust (see Pies).

Put the pitted dates, the coconut nectar mixture and the two oranges (using peels also) through the food chopper. Set this mixture aside, then flake 1/4 lb. pine nuts. Grind six pared apples into the pine nuts,

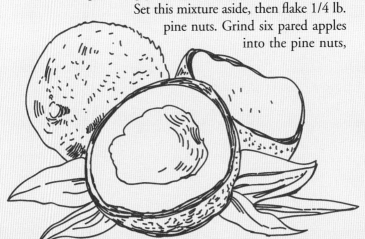

thoroughly mixing into the nuts as you grind the apples, which will prevent them turning dark.

Now spread your pie crust with half of the coconut-date mixture, take off the plate and lay pie crust on flat surface. Next spread on the apple-pine nut mixture, moulding into cake shape with your fingers. Then cut the pie crust in half and spread the other half with the remaining coconut-date mixture.

Now lay the second half-pie crust on top of the first half, then powder the whole with shredded coconut, or finish the top by spreading on a mixture of carob powder, coconut nectar and flaked pine nuts. Slice the cake with a sharp knife, cutting in about ten slices.

Christmas Spice Cake

1 lb. black dried figs, 1 lb. pitted dates, 1 lb. pitted prunes, 1/2 lb. seedless raisins. Put these dried fruits through the food chopper, then add two pounds whole walnuts and 1/2 lb. whole seedless raisins. Now work in as much oatmeal (made by grinding up rolled oats) as the above mixture will hold, moistening slightly with corn oil and flavoring with a little grated orange peel and pastry spice. Mix all ingredients well, then press into cake mould.

Oatmeal Cookies

Equal parts flaked cashew nuts and oatmeal (made by grinding up rolled oats); a sprinkling of seedless raisins. Flavor to taste with pastry spice (editor's note:

you can combine cinnamon, ground cloves, cardamom and nutmeg to achieve the same aroma); then work in coconut nectar and corn oil to the consistency where it can be rolled out. Cut out cookies with your shape of choice and spread out on flat surface for several hours.

Nut Cream, Iced

1 lb. perfectly ripe, mashed bananas, 1 lb. strawberries, macerated, 1/2 lb. coconut nectar, 1/2 lb. pine nuts flaked, 1 pint of water. Mix all ingredients together (with a hand whisk or your blender of choice) until deliciously smooth. Then spoon into an airtight tub or container. Above recipe makes two litres of ice cream. Freeze for at least twelve hours (or overnight) and be sure to serve direct from the freezer.

PREMIUM QUALITY

PREMIUM
★★★
Organic
PRODUCT

100% NATURAL

Sweet
Strawberry

Pies

Cherry

All-Purpose Pie Crust

3 oz. seedless raisins, 2 oz. whole wheat meal. Put the raisins through food chopper and work into them the wheat meal. Roll out thinly and mould in pie plate, trimming off edge with knife. Expose to the sunshine to dry. Pie crust for eight- or nine-inch pie plate should weigh four or five ounces. Pie filling should weigh one pound.

Red Raspberry Pie

Mash up 3/4 lb. of ripe red raspberries and sweeten slightly by adding a little coconut nectar. Slice lengthwise into your pie crust a ripe banana, fully covering the bottom, sprinkle lightly with flaked almonds, and then fill the pie crust with the crushed raspberries, smoothing the top with a knife and garnishing around edge with perfect whole berries; also place a berry in the center of each slice. This pie should be cut and served up on individual plates,

as soon as possible
after making.

Strawberry Pie
Is made the same as the
raspberry, substituting
strawberries.

Banana Pie
Select fully ripe bananas. Slice length-wise into pie crust,
fully covering it. Now sprinkle lightly a few finely ground
nuts over this and add another layer of sliced bananas,
filling the pie crust. Drizzle with a little coconut nectar
and sprinkle with finely ground nuts.

Apple Banana Pie
Mash with a fork two ripe bananas, removing all lumps.
Add 6 oz. grated apple and 4 oz. flaked almonds. Mix to
an even consistency and spoon into pie crust.

Apple Cream Pie
12 oz. grated apple, 4 oz.
flaked pine nuts. Mix well
and use to fill in pie crust,
smoothing the top over so that
it may be garnished with a few
whole pine nuts, apple slices or
seedless raisins.

Prune Pie

Soak the prunes overnight, drain and remove pits, chop the pulp finely and mix with flaked pine nuts, the proportion being 11 oz. chopped prunes to 5 oz. flaked pine nuts. Fill in crust and garnish top with a few whole pine nuts, pressing them into the filling.

Mock Cherry Pie

Mix together 10 oz. seedless raisins and 6 oz. red ripe cranberries which have been washed and drained well. Run through food chopper and sweeten with coconut nectar, mixing well together and fill in pie crust.

Celery Cream Pie

9 oz. finely minced celery (tender stalks only should be used), 5 oz. finely chopped apple, 2 oz. flaked peanuts or pine nuts. Mix all ingredients well together, sweeten to taste with coconut nectar and spoon into pie crust.

Pumpkin Pie

10 oz. grated pumpkin or squash, 5 oz. either flaked peanuts or pine nuts. Mix well together

with a pinch
of nutmeg, add a
tablespoonful of coconut
nectar and mix again. Spoon into
pie crust and sprinkle with a dusting of
ground cinnamon.

Date Pie
Put pitted dates through food chopper, and to 12 oz. of
the ground fruit add 4 oz. mashed banana. Mix well and
spoon into pie crust.

Fig Pie
Is made the same as above, substituting black dried figs
for the dates.

Mince Pie
5 oz. finely chopped apple, 5 oz. raisins, 3 oz. dates, 3
oz. black dried figs. Cut the figs into pieces and mix
the dried fruits thoroughly together, then run through
food chopper. Now add the chopped apple and blend
all ingredients thoroughly, flavoring with a pinch of

cinnamon, one of nutmeg and a little dried grated orange peel. Sweet-toothed chefs should add a little coconut nectar to the mix. Fill in pie crust and crimp edge with a fork.

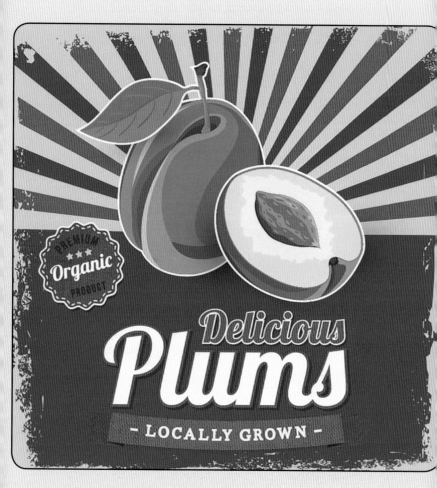

Confections

Carob Confection

Stir 4 oz. pine nuts into 1 lb. carob powder, adding a generous helping of coconut nectar to bind the mixture together. Mix thoroughly, roll out and cut into squares.

Coconut Caramels

Work shredded coconut into two cups of chilled and slightly solidified date paste, until the mixture becomes stiff enough to roll out. Cut into generous squares, wrap in waxed paper and prepare to serve. (Editor's note: Vera's original recipe calls for candied or solidified honey, but chilled date paste is probably the closest vegan equivalent. To make your own, pack two cups of dates into a single glass jar, pressing them together quite closely. Cover them with water and leave to soak and soften overnight. Next morning, transfer the entire contents of the jar to your

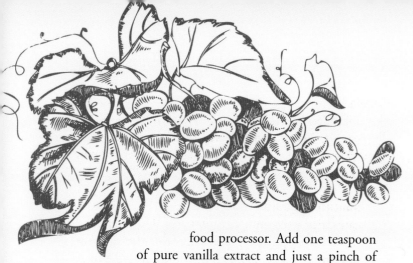

food processor. Add one teaspoon of pure vanilla extract and just a pinch of Himalayan salt to taste. Process for five to ten minutes until you've achieved a deliciously creamy paste. Spoon back into glass jar and store in the fridge, where your paste will have a shelf-life of up to three months.)

Coconut-Raisin Caramel

1 lb. seedless raisins, 1/4 lb. shredded coconut. Mix well and run through food chopper. Roll out and cut into squares.

Raisin Balls

Run 1 lb. seedless raisins through food chopper. Form into 2 oz. balls and roll in coconut.

Peanut Butter Confection

1 lb. dates, 1 tablespoon peanut butter. Put dates through food chopper using fine cutter and work into them the peanut butter. Roll out and cut into squares.

Figola

1 1/2 lbs. dried black figs, 1/4 lb. pitted dried olives, 1/4 lb. peanuts. Mix ingredients well together, run through food chopper, roll out and cut into squares, then wrap in waxed paper.

Fig-Almond Confection

1 lb. sun-dried white figs, 2 oz. almonds, 1/4 lb. almond butter. Cut the figs into pieces, mix with the almonds and run through food chopper; then work into the mass the almond butter, mixing thoroughly. Roll out and cut into squares.

Figgy-Walnut Confection

1 lb. dried black figs and 1 lb. walnuts run through food chopper, using fine cutter. Mix, roll out and cut into squares, which may then be wrapped in waxed paper.

Prune-Walnut Confection

1 lb. pitted prunes, 1 lb. dates and 6 oz. walnuts. Mix together and run through food chopper, roll out and cut into squares.

Chop-Sticks

3 lbs. seeded dates, 1/4 lb. walnuts, 1/4 lb. shredded coconut, 1/2 lb. dried bananas.

Cut the bananas in inch-long pieces, mix all ingredients well together and run through food chopper, using fine cutter. Roll into sticks 4 inches long, which should be wrapped in waxed paper.

Stuffed Dates

Remove pits from a box of your favorite seeded dates, taking care not to mangle them. Fill with walnuts, pecans or your own homemade date paste (see Coconut Caramels for the recipe). Prunes may be treated the same way.

Pecan Patties

4 oz. each figs, dates, raisins and coconut nectar, 2 oz. each walnuts and pecans. Cut figs into pieces, mix dried fruits and nuts thoroughly together and run through food chopper, then add the coconut nectar, blending well into the mixture. Roll out, cut into squares and wrap in waxed paper.

Plum Pudding

1 oz. each dried figs, pitted dates and prunes, 2 oz. raisins, 1 oz. walnuts or pecans. Mix all ingredients together, then run through food chopper. Add a pinch of cinnamon, nutmeg and grated dried orange peel, folding well into

the mixture, and form into a pudding shape (editor's note: molding into a rounded bowl is one way to achieve this). During the holiday season, these can be tied with festive Christmas ribbon.

CONVERSION CHART

1 pinch = less than 1/8 teaspoon (dry) = 0.5 grams
1 dash = 3 drops to ¼ teaspoon (liquid) = 1.25 grams
1 teaspoon (liquid) = 5.0 grams
3 teaspoons = 1 tablespoon = ½ ounce = 14.3 grams
2 tablespoons = 1 ounce = 28.35 grams
4 tablespoons = 2 ounces = ¼ cup = 56.7 grams
8 tablespoons = 4 ounces = ½ cup = 113.4 grams
8 tablespoons (flour) = about 2 ounces = 72.0 grams
16 tablespoons = 8 ounces = 1 cup = ½ pound = 226.8 grams
32 tablespoons = 16 ounces = 2 cups = 1 pound = 453.6 grams
64 tablespoons = 32 ounces = 1 quart = 2 pounds = 907.0 grams

Oats: 1 cup = 100 grams
Nuts: 1 cup = 125 grams
Honey/Coconut Nectar: 1 cup = 350 grams
Pitted Dried Dates: 1 cup = 175 grams
Raisins and Sultanas: 1 cup = 150 grams
Nut Butter: 1 cup = 250 grams
Flour: 1 cup = 125 grams
Water: 1 cup = 240 millilitres

ACKNOWLEDGEMENTS

Mrs Vera Richter self-published the world's first vegan raw food cookbook in 1925 under the title, *Mrs Richter's Cook-less Book*. The title remained in print until 1944. This version of her original cookbook has been adapted and updated for a modern audience by Laura Coulman. However the book remains essentially as it was first written, apart from a few alternatives to those ingredients of a far-off period. All of the illustrations have been added to this edition by the Publisher.

Research into the lives and work of Dr John and Mrs Vera Richter has been helped by the following articles, books and websites: *Hollywood Dish: More Than 150 Delicious, Healthy Recipes from Hollywood's Chef to the Stars* by Akasha Richmond; Philip Lovell, 1928 *https://restaurant-ingthroughhistory.com/2014/02/02/back-to-nature-the-eutropheon*; Jan Whitaker: *Back to Nature: The Eutropheon https://restaurant-ingthroughhistory.com/2014/02/02/back-to-nature-the-eutropheon/*; Gordon Kennedy: *http://www.sunfood.net/johnrichter.html*; Rynn Berry, *Satya* Magazine: http://www.satyamag.com/june03/berry.html; http://frieze-magazin.de/archiv/features/kalifornication/?lang=en; *The Oxford Encyclopedia of Food and Drink in America, Volume 2* by Andrew Smith; *Becoming Raw: The Essential Guide to Raw Vegan Diets* by Brenda Davis and Vesanto Melina; *Eating in the Raw* by Carol Alt; http://www.alkalineliving.net/raw-food-history.html; *California Health News*, 1941.